Elizabeth I

A Cherrytree Book

Designed and produced by
A S Publishing

First published 1989
by Cherrytree Press Ltd
a subsidiary of
The Chivers Company Ltd
Windsor Bridge Road,
Bath, Avon BA2 3AX

Copyright © Cherrytree Press Ltd 1989

British Library Cataloguing in Publication Data

Frost, Abigail
    Elizabeth I.
    1. England. Elizabeth I. Queen of England
    I. Title II. Greene, Gwen III. Series
    942.05'5'0924

ISBN 0-7451-5030-6

Printed in Hong Kong by Colorcraft Ltd

CHILDREN OF HISTORY

Elizabeth I

By Abigail Frost · *Illustrated by* Gwen Green

CHERRYTREE BOOKS

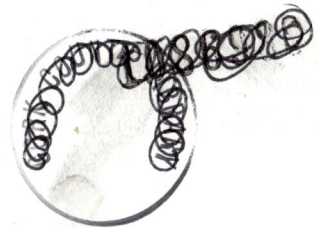

King Henry's Daughter

THE TUDOR
SUCCESSION
We call Elizabeth's family
the Tudor dynasty, after
her grandfather Henry VII.
Her father Henry VIII
was the second Tudor
king, and feared he might
be the last. It was a king's
duty to his people to make
the succession to the
throne certain. Henry's
own father had come to the
throne after years of
bloody civil war between
different claimants, and
nobody wanted to see such
times again. Henry feared
that unless he had a son –
one who would be a grown
man when his father died –
there was a serious risk
that the horrors of civil war
would return.

At three in the afternoon on Sunday 7 September 1533, the city of London was peaceful and quiet. But far on its outskirts, beside the River Thames in the east, one grand house was alive with busy people – and those who were not busy were anxious and watchful. For this was King Henry VIII's palace at Greenwich, and in an upper room Anne Boleyn, the Queen of England, was giving birth to a child who would one day inherit his throne.

Anne and Henry were certain the baby would be a boy – the next King of England. Their astrologers had predicted that they would have what they wanted. Henry had already divorced one wife because she seemed unable to bear a boy child who lived.

Henry's Divorce

Henry's first wife, Catherine of Aragon, had had a daughter, Mary, now an intelligent girl of 17. But it was almost unthinkable in those days that a woman could rule a rich and powerful country; and Mary had another disadvantage. Like her mother, she was a Catholic. And Henry, unable to get the Pope to agree to his divorce, had broken away from the Catholic Church and taken his country with him.

So all the hopes of king and country were set upon the baby boy the astrologers had told them to expect. But even kings and astrologers cannot tell nature what to do, and the baby was a girl. The celebration bonfires that the people had planned were not lit. Yet the little girl did in the end rule England; her reign was long, and the country was powerful, peaceful and prosperous during it. We know her today as Queen Elizabeth I.

Anne was tired after the long birth, but happy. The future seemed bright for the beautiful young Queen. But Henry found it hard to hide his disappointment that the baby was not a son.

A Princess's Progress

TUDOR CHILDREN
Baby Elizabeth travelled with a wet-nurse – a country woman who suckled great ladies' babies so that they did not have to do it themselves. People of her time did not like the mess and noise of tiny children. Babies were wrapped from head to foot in swaddling cloths – strips of linen rather like those on an ancient Egyptian mummy. They look like peg-dolls in paintings. The swaddling acted like a modern nappy – though it was not changed as often.

Though Henry and Anne had not had the son they hoped for, Anne was not worried. It seemed that there was plenty of time for a son to be born. Their daughter Elizabeth was christened in Greenwich Church by the Bishop of London, watched by the Lord Mayor and other important people.

Elizabeth's christening robe was purple velvet and the font was made of silver, with a red satin canopy fringed with gold. She had a duchess for a godmother, and the Archbishop of Canterbury for her godfather. But one person was missing at this grand occasion – Elizabeth's father. Some people whispered that the christening was 'very cold and disagreeable to the court and to the city'. Perhaps Henry was already beginning to have second thoughts about his marriage to Anne.

To the Country

While still a tiny baby, Elizabeth was taken to live in the country and be brought up by a foster-mother, Lady Bryan. There was plague in London, and it was no place for a child to grow up healthy. Elizabeth's first country home was Hatfield Palace, to the north-east of London, but like other members of the Royal family she had several homes, and would move from palace to palace in a stately procession called a progress.

Elizabeth rode with her nurse on a litter. Behind her rode her servants, *their* servants, and the household's clothes, gold and silver plate, and other possessions, which were carried on horse-drawn wagons. When night fell, they would descend upon the greatest house in the neighbourhood – and the owner would have to feed and house them all in great style for as long as they wanted.

The progress moved slowly, covering as little as ten or fifteen miles a day. Elizabeth continued this custom all her life. Her Royal Progresses were famous for the honour they gave their hosts, the great entertainments given for the Queen – and the terrible drain they were on the purses of the lords they visited. One of her progresses included more than 300 wagons.

The King's Great Matter

KING AGAINST POPE
Henry's divorce was a complicated matter. Catholics could not be divorced – as they may not to this day – unless they could prove that their marriage was not legal in the eyes of the Church. Henry's first wife, Catherine of Aragon, had been married to his brother Arthur, who died young; under the laws of the Church, this made her effectively Henry's sister – so that it was a sin for them to marry. The Pope had granted them special permission; but as the years passed, and Catherine had sons who died as babies, Henry wondered if this was God's punishment. He hired the greatest lawyers of the day to write to the Pope, arguing that his marriage was illegal; but the Pope refused to give him what he wanted. So he set up his own church in England, with himself as its head.

Lady Bryan, who was a cousin of Anne's, had looked after Elizabeth's half-sister Mary for many years. With a more favoured child in the family, Mary was insultingly treated. Henry sent orders that Mary was to bow her knee to the baby princess, and be her maid of honour. Mary said haughtily that she knew no other princess but herself, but would agree to call the baby 'sister'. Henry responded by ordering Lady Shelton, who ran Elizabeth's household, to beat Mary if she were troublesome. The two sisters treated each other coolly for the rest of their lives.

A Grand Father

The princesses' father Henry was a king on a grand scale. When he broke with the Catholic Church, he had seized all the lands belonging to the wealthy monasteries of England and was now immensely rich. He spent much of the money on building and enlarging palaces, bringing fine craftsmen from France and Italy to decorate them in the very latest styles. England had never seen such magnificence. He loved to eat and drink, and held the greatest banquets of the age. He liked to hunt and to ride and fight mock battles in the tilt-yard; but he had more delicate talents, too. Many people think he wrote the sad song *Greensleeves:*

> Alas, my love, you do me wrong,
>   To cast me off discourteously.
> For I have loved you for so long,
>   Delighting in your company.

In real life, it was Henry who did the casting off. He married six wives in all, and cast off four of them, two in a

8

Elizabeth's arrival caused problems for her sister Mary. She was forbidden to call herself princess and her servants could no longer wear gold on their uniforms. Not surprisingly, she was jealous when Lady Bryan pampered the little child.

way which seems unimaginably brutal today. He ordered their heads to be cut off, and it was Elizabeth's mother Anne who was to be the first to suffer this horrible fate.

He had ended his first marriage because he became convinced that it was sinful, and under a curse. People called his divorce – and his quarrel with the Pope about it – 'the King's great matter'. Now Anne, too, had failed to give him a male heir. Was the curse still with him?

Elizabeth had never seen such sights. The great banqueting hall of Whitehall Palace was filled with dancing gentlemen and ladies. Musicians moved among them, playing the King's favourite tunes. Her father held her high up so that she had a good view, and everyone who passed was made to admire her.

Triumphs and Tears

Baby Elizabeth hardly had a chance to know her mother, but her mother thought of her. Elizabeth slept in a cradle decorated with crimson and satin fringes, chosen by Anne, and wore white and purple caps with gold embroidery which Anne had had made. When her hair grew long, Anne sent ribbons to curl it in.

Anne's own life was a round of parties. As the year 1536 began, everything seemed in her favour. She was expecting another baby – the hoped-for prince, perhaps – and then

Catherine of Aragon died. Henry and Anne did not disguise their glee. Great feasts were ordered to celebrate, and their two-year-old daughter travelled to London to join in. It was Elizabeth's first real sight of the splendour of her father's court. Henry, dressed all over in yellow, took her to chapel 'with trumpets and other great triumphs.' She sat at dinner in his banqueting hall, and afterwards he carried her around in his arms for all the courtiers to see. For Elizabeth, it was the most exciting day of her short life. Perhaps, even then, she vowed that her own court one day would be as splendid. Certainly, as Queen, she shared Henry's love of fine clothes, dancing and pageantry.

Anne, too, must have been proud and full of hope for the future. But within a month, she had had a still-born son – and Henry had remembered the curse he feared.

Anne Falls From Favour

The Boleyns, Anne's family, had come to great power when she became Queen, and of course they had made enemies. Now these enemies saw their chance. Dreadful stories were spread about – that she had had other lovers, even that Elizabeth was not Henry's true child. Meanwhile, Henry had fallen in love with Jane Seymour, who came from another powerful family at court. Anne was tried for treason, and sent to the Tower of London to await execution. Elizabeth made another journey to London – not knowing it was to see her mother for the last time.

The day before Anne went to prison, she was seen at a high window of Greenwich Palace, pleading tearfully with her husband while she cuddled Elizabeth. In May she was beheaded at the Tower, and the very next day Henry was formally betrothed to Jane Seymour. Now it was Elizabeth's turn to lose the title of princess.

Elizabeth clung to her weeping mother, aware only that something dreadful was happening. She had never seen her father in such a terrible mood. Whatever her mother said to him, he only became more angry. She never saw Anne again.

Neither Gown nor Kirtle

It was years before Elizabeth learned what had happened to her mother. But it did not affect her view of her father. Henry was always kind to Elizabeth, who adored him and thought him the model of what a ruler should be. She once told a courtier who had spoken out of turn that he would not have dared address her father so.

Though she had lost her title and the mother she hardly knew, Elizabeth felt secure. Home for her was wherever her

Lady Bryan could not keep Elizabeth away from the grown-ups' rich food. She wrote to Cromwell: 'Alas, my Lord, it is not meet [right] for a child of her age . . . I dare not take it upon me to keep her in health . . . for there she shall see divers [different kinds of] meats and fruits, and wine, which would be hard for me to restrain Her Grace from.'

foster-mother Lady Bryan was. Lady Bryan kept the King informed about his daughter's progress by writing to his minister Thomas Cromwell. She told him of Elizabeth's teething problems when she was a baby: 'They come very slowly forth, and cause me to suffer Her Grace to have her will more than I would'.

The pompous steward of the house insisted that Elizabeth must eat with the grown-ups, and Lady Bryan thought this was bad for her. Henry sent instructions that Elizabeth was to have simple food in her own room.

Worst of all, for Lady Bryan, Elizabeth had outgrown all her clothes: 'She hath neither gown nor kirtle, nor no manner of linen, nor foresmocks, nor kerchiefs, nor rails, nor bodystichets, nor handkerchiefs . . .'. New clothes came from London.

A Baby Brother

Toothache, special food, new clothes; these were the important things for Elizabeth. The great events of the court hardly affected her life. But one event Elizabeth knew all about – the arrival of her baby half-brother, the future king.

Poor Queen Jane had given Henry the son he so desperately wanted – at the cost of her own life. She died soon after Prince Edward's birth, probably of an infection. Many women died that way at the time. Elizabeth travelled to Hampton Court to take part in Edward's christening and the celebrations that went with it – the first time she took part in a public ceremony. She was only four. Dressed in her best, with a heavy embroidered train, she carried Edward's christening robe in the procession into the palace chapel. The robe was heavy, covered with embroidery and jewels, so one of the courtiers had to carry *her*.

Elizabeth was fascinated by her baby brother, especially when he wore his lovely christening robe. It seemed strange that this tiny person was the second most important of the kingdom – for he would be King like their father one day.

In the Country

The little prince joined Elizabeth and Mary with Lady Bryan, and inevitably took up most of his foster-mother's attention. Elizabeth sewed him a little shirt, trying hard to make the stitches neat. Already, at an age when modern children have not started school, she was learning to sew, to read and write, and to play musical instruments. Mary – more friendly now – taught her card games.

While Elizabeth was living in the country, her father married again – three times in all. Elizabeth was ten when he married his last wife, Catherine Parr. She was a widow, and a very kind and learned woman, who told Henry it was time his children came to live at court.

CATHERINE PARR
Henry's last wife was in her early thirties when they were married. She did not marry him out of choice, but once they were married she was a good and conscientious Queen, kind to her step-children and her elderly husband. When Henry went off to war in France in 1544, she ruled the country until he returned.

Though Edward, as heir to the throne, was expected to go to court and take part in formal occasions, at home with Elizabeth he could romp about like any little boy.

HOUSEHOLD ENTERTAINMENTS

Besides Elizabeth, Mary and Edward, Lady Bryan and the various officials and servants, the Royal children's household included entertainers – among them a fool, or jester, called Jane and a tumbler called Lucretia. The children laughed at their funny antics, but there was a more serious reason for keeping jesters. They were there to remind their great masters that they were human. Henry VIII's jester, Will Somers, could get away with telling the King all sorts of things he would rather not know.

Musicians were part of any great household; they would play while the family ate their meals, and afterwards for dancing. Lady Bryan describes the two-year-old Edward dancing in one of her letters: 'His Grace danced and played so wantonly that he could not stand still, and was as full of pretty toys as ever I saw a child in my life.'

A Scholar at Court

Catherine Parr took a special interest in Elizabeth, who loved reading and foreign languages just as she did. She arranged for her to be taught by the most learned scholars of Cambridge University.

Elizabeth's studies were a heavy load for a ten-year-old. As well as Latin, she mastered the New Testament in Greek, and learned French and Italian – the languages of international diplomats. Her other reading was expected to be very serious. She could read stories from history, classical mythology and the Bible – but romances and other lightweight stories were banned.

Courtly Entertainment

Elizabeth did not need to read about knights and ladies – they were all around her at home. Life at court was colourful enough. Elizabeth loved to watch important foreign visitors arriving at Whitehall Palace, comparing their rich clothes with the English fashions. Guests were entertained in the evenings with a banquet, and often a masque. This was a cross between a play, a ballet, and a pageant, acted by the King and his courtiers, dressed up as mythological characters.

The most exciting of the court entertainments was tilting. Two knights, in decorated armour, would ride in mock battle on either side of a barrier. The winner had to unseat the other with his lance. Tilting had started long before Henry's day as fighting practice for knights. Now guns had taken over from lances and swords in real battles, and tilting was carried on as sport. Elizabeth herself learnt to ride well, and also learnt archery. She enjoyed these sports, but did not care so much for her other lessons in embroidery.

Roger Ascham, who taught
Elizabeth Latin, remained
her tutor even when she
was Queen.

A Gift for a Queen

As a New Year's gift to Catherine, whom she had grown to love like a mother, Elizabeth carefully translated the Queen's own prayers into Latin, French and Italian, and copied them out in beautiful italic handwriting. Catherine was delighted at this proof of her step-daughter's learning. Unfortunately, her writing was not always as good when she grew up. One historian complains that she had the most illegible handwriting of any English monarch!

Elizabeth loved her riding lessons in Richmond Park, the King's hunting-ground to the south-west of London. All her life she enjoyed riding and hunting with her courtiers. She also learnt to shoot arrows at the archery butts there.

A Boy King

In 1547, Elizabeth's father died. It was three days before she – or anyone else but his closest ministers – was told about it. She and her little brother were staying at Eltham Palace when they learnt that he was now King Edward VI. He was only nine. Elizabeth wrote him a formal letter of condolence, saying that she would bear her bereavement like a Christian and a philosopher. Of course, she was sad that her father was dead, but she believed that he had gone to Heaven, and she looked forward to a long and happy reign for Edward, who, like her, was a staunch Protestant.

Intrigues at Court

Why did she not hear of Henry's death at once? The reason was politics. Henry's ministers needed a little time to make arrangements for Edward's reign. Clever though he was, he was far too young to rule alone. In the past, when small boys had come to the throne, one of their relations had ruled on their behalf, being known as a Lord Protector. But these had not been happy times. Before his death Henry decided that it would be better to have the country ruled for a time by a Council of trusted ministers. The ministers he chose wanted everything set up properly before the people heard they had a new King. But despite their efforts, Edward's uncle, Lord Edward Seymour, Duke of Somerset, quickly managed to establish himself as Lord Protector – the most powerful man in the land.

Elizabeth's own position had changed too. At 13, she was thought old enough to marry. As the King's sister, and third in line to the throne, she would bring great power and influence to the man she married.

When Edward became King, his main concern was the Church. He ordered the writing of the first prayer books in English, and had his own personal preachers at court.

Time for Marriage?

Almost immediately, and unbeknown to her, Elizabeth had a suitor – the Lord Protector's brother Lord Thomas Seymour. Seymour's 'courtship' consisted of asking discreetly around the court what his brother would think of the marriage. The answer was always that he would not allow it. So Seymour settled for the next best marriage – to Catherine Parr.

Catherine, who had three times been married to old men,

Chelsea is now part of central London, but then it was in the country. It was a fashionable place to live, with its fresh air and lovely gardens. As Elizabeth sat in those gardens, Seymour

would pay attention to her. Sometimes he would tickle her, or even give her hugs and kisses. Elizabeth's lace sunhat still exists – it is kept at Hatfield House, near her childhood home.

was delighted to get a proposal from a handsome man near her own age, and fell head-over-heels in love. They married quickly, and went to live in a house in Chelsea which Henry had left Catherine in his will. Elizabeth, knowing nothing of Seymour's plots behind the scenes, went with them, happy to continue her education with her beloved step-mother.

Elizabeth in Disgrace

Though married to Catherine, Seymour paid court to the young Elizabeth. Friendly gestures would turn into teasing games or even outright flirtation. Elizabeth blushed, and tried to fend him off, but secretly she enjoyed these games. Catherine Parr joined in at first, thinking it all harmless fun, but later she changed her mind. One day she caught Seymour holding Elizabeth in his arms. That was enough – Elizabeth was sent packing that very day. Off she went to Hertfordshire, with her governess Kate Ashley and her tutor Roger Ascham. Ascham set her back on course with her studies. She wrote letters in Latin to her brother the King, and had her portrait painted to send him.

Later that year came the sad news that Catherine had died in childbirth.

A Lesson in Love

By now word of Seymour's many plots had come to his brother's ears, and he was tried for treason. Elizabeth's trusted servants were harshly questioned about his games with her. In the end he was beheaded.

Elizabeth learnt a lot from this sad episode. She realised that she had been a foolish girl, playing at love with another woman's husband. She now knew that, in her position, men might play with her feelings in order to get her power for themselves.

21

A Catholic Queen

NINE DAYS' QUEEN
Lady Jane Grey was the great-granddaughter of Henry VII. Powerful men at court persuaded Edward that this clever, quiet young woman – whom they could control – should succeed him rather than his sister Mary, who would return the nation to Catholicism. After the King's death, Jane, who was only 16, was installed on the throne, to be deposed nine days later by Mary, the rightful heir.

Sensibly, Elizabeth kept well out of the way of these events. Poor Jane was taken to the Tower of London, charged with treason and beheaded.

Everyone had expected a long reign for Edward VI. But he had never been strong, and at 15 he caught the deadly disease tuberculosis. News of his illness was kept from Elizabeth by scheming ministers who wanted to put their own candidate on the throne when he died. At last they summoned her to her brother's death-bed. But Elizabeth suspected that they really wanted to capture her, and so she sent word that she was too ill to travel. She waited at Hatfield while Edward died, the plot failed, and her sister Mary was proclaimed Queen. Then she wrote to Mary, congratulating her and asking to come and pay homage.

Mary, who was in Suffolk, rode towards London and met Elizabeth at Wanstead. Elizabeth knelt to her sister, and was received with grace. Then she rode in Mary's procession to the Tower of London, where it was traditional for a new King or Queen to spend the night, as a sign of taking possession of the city. They were followed by five thousand country people, and the route was lined with cheering crowds.

Ordered to Mass

The sisters' new friendship was short-lived. Mary set about restoring the Catholic Church, and started by ordering everyone at court to go to Mass. Elizabeth did not go. Mary summoned her to her room and asked why.

Elizabeth tried to stall, explaining that she had been brought up a Protestant, and knew nothing of 'the doctrine of ancient religion'. Mary was not fooled, and insisted that her stubborn sister should go to Mass the very next week.

On Sunday, messengers arrived at Elizabeth's door to make sure she went to the service. Elizabeth claimed to be ill. When this did not get her excused from Mass, she went along to the chapel, complaining all the way of a stomach ache. Mary lost her temper, but dared not do too much against Elizabeth, the heir to the throne. Mary's popularity with the people was waning fast. She agreed to let Elizabeth go to the country, where her religion would not offend the Queen's own views.

As Mary led the way to the chapel for Mass, Elizabeth clutched her stomach and complained loudly of a pain. Her sister recognised this for the trick it was, and took no notice.

Against the Tide

Both sisters were relieved to part. Elizabeth could quietly worship as she chose, and Mary could now concentrate on her coming marriage to King Philip of Spain. But the people did not want their Queen to marry a Spaniard.

Elizabeth, at her country house, had some sinister visitors – the leaders of various rebel groups. They wanted to depose Mary and make Elizabeth Queen. She listened to their plans, but was too clever to do anything which might seem like approving them.

Only one of the planned rebellions took place. Its leader, Sir Thomas Wyatt, led an army towards London, demanding that Mary should not marry Philip. Mary ordered Elizabeth back to London so she could keep her eye on her. Elizabeth again pleaded that she was too ill to obey.

Mary Saves her Crown

With rebels at London's gates, Mary addressed the people. She said she loved them like a mother, and reminded them how they had sworn allegiance at her coronation. Thousands joined her army to defeat the rebels. Mary, now safe, sent doctors to see if Elizabeth had told the truth when she said she was ill. They said she had, but she was now well enough to travel. Mary ordered her to court. As she set out, Elizabeth was afraid she was going to the executioner's block. She stayed four weeks in Whitehall Palace, watched all the time, as the rebels were questioned.

Still suspecting her sister of treason, Mary decided to send Elizabeth to the Tower. On 16 March, just after Wyatt's trial, she sent two lords to take Elizabeth there. She was to travel by water; the streets were too risky. Elizabeth did not believe Mary had ordered this, and begged to see

her. The lords refused. She asked to write a letter; one lord said no, but the other said she might.

This was Elizabeth's chance. She often travelled down the Thames, and knew it was too dangerous to row under London Bridge at high tide. If she could spin out her letter, she might win time to see Mary and regain her freedom. She wrote slowly at first, but became agitated later, leaving out words and making spelling mistakes. As she finished, she glanced out at the river; the tide was high. She had won another day out of the Tower.

Elizabeth strung out her letter to Mary for as long as she could. A third of the way down the second page she had said all that she could say; but she dared not risk leaving a blank space, which might be used to add a forged 'confession' of guilt. So she drew diagonal lines across the sheet.

Two Prisons

Next day the lords came again. Mary had scolded them for letting Elizabeth outwit them. They led her to the river, and the lonely ride to the Tower.

Soldiers waited there. Remembering her mother's death, Elizabeth feared for her own life. 'Oh Lord,' she said, 'I never thought to have come here as a prisoner!' (She had expected to stay there before her coronation.)

Despite its grim history, the Tower was a comfortable prison. Prisoners had their own furniture, and their favourite meals were brought in. You can still see their names carved on the walls. Elizabeth was well treated – her door was not even locked. She liked to walk in the lieutenant's garden, where children brought her flowers and presents.

In May, Mary decided to move her. Once again Elizabeth was rowed along the Thames, and the rumour spread quickly that she had been set free. At first Elizabeth was

The tide was running high, and Elizabeth's feet got wet coming ashore. She entered the Tower through a low, barred gate from the river, which still exists and is now known as 'Traitor's Gate'. She begged everyone there to witness that 'I come in no traitor, but as true a woman to the Queen's Majesty as any is now living.'

afraid again. For four days she rode through country lanes, not knowing her destination. But all the way, the people came out to cheer. She began to feel like a queen.

At last she reached Woodstock, an old, half-ruined palace near Oxford. Only four rooms were fit to live in. Armed guards stood on a nearby hill, in case rebels tried to set her free. Elizabeth felt anxious, not knowing what would happen to her or even why she was there.

In the spring, Mary sent for Elizabeth, to face more questions at Hampton Court. Late one night, one of Mary's ladies came and led Elizabeth by torchlight through the dark palace to the Queen's room. Elizabeth knelt, and said she was innocent. This time Mary believed her. After a long talk, the warring sisters were at peace; and so they remained until November 1558, when Mary died.

At every village Elizabeth rode through, the people came to cheer. At High Wycombe women gave her cakes – so many that she had to ask them to stop, because there was not enough room in her litter. Bells were rung and musicians played to celebrate her progress through the country.

A Popular Coronation

CORONATION FINERY

Elizabeth spent a fortune on coronation finery. Her own dresses were the most magnificent ever seen. Everyone at court had new clothes, even the jesters, who were splendid in orange velvet with purple and gold trimmings. Lord Robert Dudley, Elizabeth's Master of Horse, bought cloth of gold, velvets and satin; ostrich feathers for helmets; spangles of silver and gold for the guardsmen's coats; and cloth of silver to cover the Queen's ceremonial chair. New litters and carriages were ordered for the procession, and red velvet saddles for those who rode on horseback. When Dudley did his accounts, he found that it had all cost £16,741 19s 8¾d – which would be over a million pounds today!

All the bells of London rang for the new Queen. But Elizabeth cried for the death of Mary, the last of her own family; at 25, she was all alone. She was also the most powerful woman in the world. She rode to London to set up her government and arrange her coronation.

There was little time for preparation – just two months. Elizabeth wanted to be safely crowned – and splendidly. She ordered the customs officers to seize all crimson silk at the ports. Her coronation clothes and her courtiers' were using up all the rich cloth in England. She wanted first pick of the finest stuff before the merchants got it.

Elizabeth's coronation processions lasted for days. First she went to the Tower in triumph. Next she rode in state through the City. Her household staff, bishops and lords rode in front; with her were heralds and knights; her ladies and the royal guards followed. Elizabeth often stopped to speak to the crowd along the way. At one stop a poor woman gave her a branch of rosemary; she kept it all the way to Westminster Abbey.

Coronation day was cold and frosty. A rich blue carpet had been laid between Westminster Hall and the Abbey door for the Queen to walk upon. But it did not last long – the crowd took every scrap for souvenirs.

Trumpets sounded as Elizabeth was crowned. After a long service, when all the lords of England paid homage, she held a great banquet, lasting until one in the morning. An armoured knight rode in on a huge horse and threw down his glove, as a challenge to anyone who denied her right to the throne. No-one dared take it up. Elizabeth was undisputed Queen at last.

As Elizabeth passed, the crowd fell upon the carpet her feet had touched, and cut it into pieces for souvenirs. The poor Duchess of Norfolk, who walked behind, was tripped up and fell to the ground.

Heart and Stomach of a King

Elizabeth reigned for 45 years. In all that time she never married. Her reign was a great age for the arts, the sciences and for exploration. William Shakespeare was only one of many great writers, whose plays were loved as much by the common people as by the Queen herself.

Elizabeth's finest hour came in 1588, when the King of Spain sent an armed navy – the Armada – to invade England. Elizabeth inspired her navy to defeat the Spanish. A tough and courageous ruler, Elizabeth could also be harsh. The year before, she had ordered the execution of her cousin Mary Stuart, the Catholic Queen of Scotland, whom some wanted to put on Elizabeth's throne.

Everything Elizabeth's father feared had come about: a child King, a return to Catholicism, albeit brief, and a woman, Elizabeth, ruling alone. Yet Elizabeth made England stronger than ever before. If he could have seen his daughter, old Henry VIII would have been proud.

In a stirring speech to her troops as they boarded ships to fight the Spanish Armada, Elizabeth offered, if necessary, to fight herself: 'to lay down for God, my kingdom, and for my people, my honour and my blood, even in the dust. I know I have but the body of a weak and feeble woman, but I have the heart and stomach of a King, and a King of England too'.

Important Events In Elizabeth's Life

1533 Born at Greenwich Palace (7 September)
1534 Henry VIII declared head of Church of England
1536 Death of Catherine of Aragon; execution of Anne Boleyn; Henry marries Jane Seymour
1537 Birth of Edward VI; death of Jane Seymour; Elizabeth takes part in Edward's christening
1539 Henry marries Anne of Cleves
1540 Henry divorces Anne of Cleves; marries Catherine Howard
1542 Catherine Howard executed
1543 Henry marries Catherine Parr; Elizabeth brought to live at court by Catherine
1547 Henry VIII dies; Edward VI ascends throne; Duke of Somerset is Lord Protector; Elizabeth moves to Chelsea
1548 Sent back to the country by Catherine; death of Catherine (September)
1553 Edward VI dies; Lady Jane Grey reigns for nine days; Mary I crowned
1554 Imprisoned following Sir Thomas Wyatt's rebellion
1555 England returns to Catholicism; Elizabeth freed and returns to Hatfield
1558 Death of Mary (17 November)
1559 Elizabeth crowned at Westminster Abbey (January); orders church services to be in English
1563 Church of England becomes established
1568-69 Imprisons her cousin, Mary Queen of Scots
1581 Knights Francis Drake after his voyage round the world
1587 Orders the execution of Mary Queen of Scots; England at war with Spain
1588 The defeat of the Spanish Armada
1599 William Shakespeare's Globe Theatre opened in London
1601 Orders execution of her former favourite, the Earl of Essex
1603 Dies at Richmond Palace (24 March)

Index